INSCRIPTIONS

ANTHONY THWAITE

INSCRIPTIONS

POEMS 1967-72

LONDON
OXFORD UNIVERSITY PRESS
NEW YORK TORONTO

1973

Oxford University Press, Ely House, London W.1

GLASGOW NEW YORK TORONTO MELBOURNE WELLINGTON
CAPE TOWN IBADAN NAIROBI DAR ES SALAAM LUSAKA ADDIS ABABA
DELHI BOMBAY CALCUTTA MADRAS KARACHI LAHORE DACCA
KUALA LUMPUR SINGAPORE HONG KONG TOKYO

ISBN 0 19 2118250

*Printed in Great Britain by
The Bowering Press, Plymouth*

for
Peter Porter

ACKNOWLEDGMENTS

SOME of these poems have appeared in *Agenda, Encounter, Humanist, Listener, The London Magazine, New Poems 1970/71, New Poems 1971/72, New Statesman, Observer, Phoenix, Poetry Book Society Christmas Supplement 1968* and *1972, Sunday Times, Times Literary Supplement, Wave, Young Winters Tales.* 'At Dunkeswell Abbey' was published by the Poem of the Month Club. 'Points' appeared as a Turret Books pamphlet. 'The Life and Death of the Pine Processionary' was commissioned as a film commentary by BBC-2 for *Horizon.* Five of the poems were first published in book form in *Penguin Modern Poets 18.* Several were broadcast by the BBC on *Poetry Now.*

CONTENTS

MONOLOGUE IN THE VALLEY
OF THE KINGS

I HAVE hidden something in the inner chamber
And sealed the lid of the sarcophagus
And levered a granite boulder against the door
And the debris has covered it so perfectly
That though you walk over it daily you never suspect.

Every day you sweat down that shaft, seeing on the walls
The paintings that convince you I am at home, living there.
But that is a blind alley, a false entrance
Flanked by a room with a few bits of junk
Nicely displayed, conventionally chosen.
The throne is quaint but commonplace, the jewels inferior,
The decorated panels not of the best period,
Though enough is there to satisfy curators.

But the inner chamber enshrines the true essence.
Do not be disappointed when I tell you
You will never find it: the authentic phoenix in gold,
The muslin soaked in herbs from recipes
No one remembers, the intricate ornaments,
And above all the copious literatures inscribed
On ivory and papyrus, the distilled wisdom
Of priests, physicians, poets and gods,
Ensuring my immortality. Though even if you found them
You would look in vain for the key, since all are in cipher
And the key is in my skull.

The key is in my skull. If you found your way
Into this chamber, you would find this last:
My skull. But first you would have to search the others,
My kinsfolk neatly parcelled, twenty-seven of them
Disintegrating in their various ways.
A woman from whose face the spices have pushed away
The delicate flaking skin: a man whose body

Seems dipped in clotted black tar, his head detached:
A hand broken through the cerements, protesting:
Mouths in rigid grins or soundless screams—
A catalogue of declensions.

How, then, do I survive? Gagged in my winding cloths,
The four brown roses withered on my chest
Leaving a purple stain, how am I different
In transcending these little circumstances?
Supposing that with uncustomary skill
You penetrated the chamber, granite, seals,
Dragged out the treasure gloatingly, distinguished
My twenty-seven sorry relatives,
Labelled them, swept and measured everything
Except this one sarcophagus, leaving that
Until the very end: supposing then
You lifted me out carefully under the arc-lamps,
Noting the gold fingernails, the unearthly smell
Of preservation—would you not tremble
At the thought of who this might be? So you would steady
Your hands a moment, like a man taking aim, and lift
The mask.
    But this hypothesis is absurd. I have told you already
You will never find it. Daily you walk about
Over the rubble, peer down the long shaft
That leads nowhere, make your notations, add
Another appendix to your laborious work.
When you die, decently cremated, made proper
By the Registrar of Births and Deaths, given by *The Times*
Your two-inch obituary, I shall perhaps
Have a chance to talk with you. Until then, I hear
Your footsteps over my head as I lie and think
Of what I have hidden here, perfect and safe.

THE ANTIQUARIAN

To reconstruct an afternoon in an antique time
Out of a broken dish, some oyster shells
And an ashy discolouration of the otherwise ochreous soil—
This is an occupation for philosophers
With more than a taste for language-problems.
It has no value beyond itself. Not even
The scrupulous cataloguing of shape, disposition, provenance
Will alleviate the strong smell of futility rising
Like a cloud of midges: the site-notebook
Is, like what it records, a disjected and maybe random
Commentary without conclusions.
                                    In a trial trench
On the excavation's southernmost flank, some young sprig
Teases a knucklebone out of a beautifully vertical
Wall, marks its cavity with a meat-skewer,
Ties to it something very like a miniature luggage-label
And drops it into a tray. Visitors observe
This performance with the set faces of persons determined
Not to be taken in; and in a sense
Their stance is a true one. Why, indeed,
Do I peer attentively at holes in roads
Or fossick about in the earth's disturbances
Or the mud of the foreshore? Imagining
Some lost groat or cup-handle will tell me
More about life than I know already,
Or simply a souvenir of luck and persistence?
I have stopped asking myself, accepting such furtive burrow-
    ings
As native to me, as mild and dim
As other people's secret traffickings.

No value, then, in these subterranean doings,
No moral to point, for once. Except I have
Some cold thought hovering here, which recognizes
The damp earthfall, the broken dish, the bone

Labelled and dropped in a tray and made to fit
In a pattern I have not guessed at yet, and may never,
But go on living with and through, no doubt.

NOTE ON THE VOYAGES

'MLK, JWH—I write them thus
Because the words must not be uttered,
Because they hold in their terse consonants
Powers unleashed by lip and tongue
To shake the already shaken frame of flesh.
Mysteries they signify, and must be hidden
However deep the chisel bites in stone
Angles and uprights , pieties of iron
Inscribed in words unyielding to the mouth.'

So we suppose the chronicler, the scribe
Schooled in his little gift, lacking invention,
Rigid in inherited dishonesties.
But how to account for more trivial fictions,
Lies of this world, fabled voyages
Beyond the straits, things seen and done there?
'Having sailed beyond the Pillars, in deep water,
We came upon a ruined temple: in it found
The limned words of our great ancestor . . .'

The scribe's forgery? Or his pleasing fantasy,
Relished by imagination, dwelt on, a mind's landfall?
How else account for such glamorous retailings
In the middle of such arid narrative?
And yet the later commentator admits
This faceless functionary 'would have had to rely
Entirely on his own imagination, and it would be
Remarkable indeed if he had succeeded, as he has,
In avoiding any mistake.'

'Forests at night—fires seen, strange music heard:
Our soothsayers warn us off. Burning rivers.
The Chariot of the Gods poised above flowing lava.
In the bay of the Southern Horn, an island of apes
Grown to be men—three females we slew,

Brought back their skins. . . . They hang now in the temple.'
Read it as allegory, fill in the interstices,
Check it against the maps: something happened,
Was lost, forgotten. And stares us in the face.

RETRACTIONS: HIPPO

Shortly before his death in A.D. *430, St. Augustine wrote his*
Retractiones, *a review of his life's work. The following year
the Vandals sacked Hippo.*

I TAKE it up and read it, and I see
Ink and papyrus melt under my gaze.
The verses blur, the luminous syllables
Lapse into darkness. In these latter days
The hills like a broken comb against the light
Scratch at each dawn and dusk, a restless music
Compounded with cicadas, crickets, flies,
Frettings of grasshoppers, the viper's hushed
Swarm down the walls and conduits: siftings, poised
As this whole town is poised, on the edge of silence.

From floor to ceiling, penitential psalms
Repeat their abject praises. Thou, Lord, art just
But justice will be done among men too,
And out beyond the walls and out at sea
Our judges gather to administer it.
Nevertheless, Thy will be done: the church
Fills with your citizens, who will not hear
My voice again, which forty years have brought
To this thin whisper. Silence claims me too.
The shelves of manuscripts entomb my tongue.

The sharp prow rose and fell into the sun,
Carrying me busily on Christ's brisk errands.
Heretics fell in disputation, laws
Were balanced on the scales of my regard.
Now at the jetty no craft waits for me
Or anyone. Again I lift the book,
And close my eyes, and see a city rise
Above all brick and marble ones. Below,
Where men are fearful and their fear is just,
A gorgon mouth yawns open and breathes fire.

AT SOUILLAC

Down the congested air, toothed beak and wing
Tear at each clinging couple stitched in stone:
Twisted within the whirlpool all go down
Where hooks and talons, fangs and pincers cling
Till the condemned are smothered, and they drown.

Outside, the air is warm, the light is clear,
The postcards concentrate on happier stuff
(A close-up of Isaiah is enough),
And nobody has anything to fear.
But something clings and will not let me off.

An allegory even saints condemn—
Ridiculous beasts and monsters, caricatures
Of evil doodled in the boring hours
When stonedust choked the throats of thirsty men—
Through that stone tunnel a dark torrent pours.

It breeds among the shadows, out of sight,
A chain of interlocking actions which,
As stone plaits over stone, and stitch with stitch,
Have nothing more to do with warmth andlight
Than a crowned virgin stained as black as pitch.

BUREAUCRAT IN RETIREMENT

WITHDRAWN, the blank prospect of years to come,
Into remoteness, a long day
Moving with this heavy river to longer night
And another day, and on till the wet clay
Covers him out of the light and he comes home.

No more action, petty notes for ignored files,
Ranks in alphabets, decisions
Trudged through for days, weeks, months,
Paper for salvage batched in scattering tons
And the desks sunk heavy under rotten piles.

Because there is no one to refer things to,
Chains of command broken, all
Confidences broken too, his acts assume
A deep unseriousness as governments fall
To men he half remembers but never knew.

Memoirs accumulate, but never his.
Vain ministers who played the fool
Dictate their vanities to secretaries
Who float up brightly through the typing pool.
He knows what keeps afloat the histories.

By the cottage wall, by the river's slow decline,
He sits and sees the fishermen.
They move hardly at all, casting their bait
Into the darkness, intent only when
Deep in the water silver backs flash and shine.

AT THE FRONTIER POST: OM

UNDER the one step up into the hut
A toad broods by the sergeant's shabby boots.
A single light bulb, acid and unshaded,
Marks out, inside, a function of the state
As well as marking where one road has ended.

Slogans ('To be on guard is half the battle')
Assure the walls if not the occupants.
Only behind a door do I catch glimpses
Of cruder appetites: a brown thigh, supple
With bourgeois blandishments, coyly entices.

Ripped from some old *Paris Match* or *Playboy*,
This functionary's unofficial decor
Cheers me a little as I sit and wait
While name and date of birth and date of entry
Are slowly copied to a dossier sheet.

Outside, between the frontier posts, the hills
Are black, unpeopled. Hours of restlessness
Seep from the silence, silt across the road.
At last the sergeant puts away his files,
Hands me my papers. And I see the toad

Hop into darkness, neutral and unstopped,
Companion of the brown-thighed girl
Hidden behind the door, beyond the frontier,
Where appetite and nature are adept
At moving quietly, or at staying still.

GHIBLI

THE sand wind makes its own long shadow
A wall of heat, a tall barrier
The candle dwindles low
The wick smothered, air
Shrunk to a leathery fist
Grasping a few dates
A sweat of sand
A fossil mist
A hand.

SIDI ABEID

The ground is mined with dead.
My foot stubs thorny snares
Over the thinly covered
Burrows of matchwood. What shares
A trench with the fat adder?
These brow-ridges, these knuckles.
By sly pitfalls I enter
The abashed pinnacles,
The horizontal towers,
Seeing the faithless contend
For the faithful in a shower
Of choked rain-glutted sand.
Thick-juiced, weeds multiply
Where nothing else can grow.
Under their trails there lie—
Indeterminate, low—
Rafters and eaves of wood
Housing Arab and Greek
In a persistent flood
Of splinters, fragments, the wreck
Salvaged from strewn lives:
The usufruct of death
Possessed by the dead. Who saves
Such exhaustions of breath
Or hopes for more shelter
Than these collapsed acres?
My snarled footsteps falter
Among the encamped travellers,
Hutments of boxed bone.
A yellow dog barks from his lair
In a dry cist. Alone
He violates silent air,
As I, bending to brush
The dust from a painted rim,
Feel the huge windless rush
Of air smother me and him.

DEAD WOOD

WORN down to stumps, shredded by the wind,
Crushed underfoot in brittle slaty husks,
The forest turned from wood to stone to dust.

The rind of bark peeled off in slivers, shed
Dry spores, mineral resins, scales of scrim,
Scattering huge-leaved branches under the sun.

These giants shrank to pigiems in the glare.
Basilisks flashed their petrifying eyes.
The whole plateau rattled with bones of trees.

Now oil-men bring the few gnarled timbers back
As souvenirs. A lopped stone branch lies there
To hold up books, or prop open a door.

AT THE ITALIAN CEMETERY, BENGHAZI

Meglior un giorno da leone che centi anni da pecora.

MUSSOLINI

THE old rhetoric inflated beyond rigour,
The Roman virtues in a cloud of sand
Blown to a mirage, detonate and roar
Like the lion, extinct since Balbo pressed the trigger
In 1936, far in the south. Here
A place of cypresses, a little Italy
Grazed by the desert wind, an enclave
For the dead, for a dead colony.
Among them all, not one unpolluted grave.
Mare Nostrum is someone else's sea.

The Mediterranean was to be a lake
Round which the imperium flourished. There came
Boatloads of dialects, music, priests,
A whole army: bushels of grain,
Cattle, tractors: archaeologists to make
The past justify the present. *Hang thirty a day
And resistance will stop. Subdue and civilize.*
The sun has flaked the neat stucco away.
Sepia fades from Cesare's, from Fabbro's eyes.
The sheep are slaughtered, the lion would not stay.

White villages were built, made ready, named
Heroically or nostalgically:
D'Annunzio, Savoia, Maddalena.
Rebels were strangled, nomads gaoled and tamed.
Dutiful bells rang across jebel and plain,
Ave Marias drowning the muezzin's cry.
Calabria, Naples, Sicily put out
Frail shoots into the hot breath of the ghibli.
Duce, Duce, the parched gullets shout,
Then the bombs fall, the echoes drift and die.

Vulgar memorials, stricken and deluded:
Marble sarcophagi, vain crucifix.
Walking here, why am I now reminded
Puzzlingly of what some cynic said:
Life is a preparation
For something that never happens? The Italian dead
Are gathered under their alien cypresses,
The path gives off its dusty exhalation,
The broken arm of an angel lifts and blesses
The lion-crazed, the shepherdless, one by one.

SURFACES

STARVED rib-cage, skeleton, the sand
Masking only fitfully what it hid:
Nothing was secret there at Sidi Abeid.
Sun bleached out bones, a dry wind
Covered and uncovered a strewn multitude.
I picked the past up like a dropped glove.
The past was naked, exposed wherever I stood
Under my feet, like a new and unfilled grave.

The oaks and chestnut trees of Richmond Park
Shake down their leaves: the path is choked with them,
Thick silt of the present, time thickening to dark
Compost: an instant history, a stream
No sooner seen than gone. Somewhere
Deep under glutted grass, packed under clay,
The past lies buried. In the loosening air
I walk through a drift of leaves that will not stay.

ODE

He enlarged the groves of the Gods, and made
For Apollo's processions, which keep his people safe,
A straight-hewn way,
Level and paved,
Sounding with the tramp of horses.
And there at the far end of the Market Place
He lies apart in death.
      PINDAR, *Pythian V* (trans. C. M. Bowra)

THERE in the agora
On the hill of Cyrene
The learned doctors
From Rome and Ann Arbor
Discovered a sepulchre
To which, being tentative,
They gave the descriptive
Name *?Tomb of Battus?*

And there indeed
It lies in the market
By the straight-hewn road
Or what little's left of it,
With busts of Hermes
Defaced in the niches
And dabs of fresh concrete
Neatly trowelled into it.

While here in the poem
For the victor ludorum,
A ritual encomium
In an out-of-date fashion,
For a moment the legendary
Stammerer, lion-tamer,
Strong city-founder,
Is briefly remembered.

Yes, I have been there
And saw it once clearly
In the sun on the hilltop
Of white-crowned Cyrene:
Yet suddenly clearer,
More real yet stranger,
Read here in England
In a few lines of Pindar.

SOLDIERS PLUNDERING A VILLAGE

Down the mud road, between tall bending trees,
Men thickly move, then fan out one by one
Into the foreground. Far left, a soldier tries
Bashing a tame duck's head in with a stick,
While on a log his smeared companion
Sits idly by a heap of casual loot—
Jugs splashing over, snatched-up joints of meat.

Dead centre, a third man has spiked a fourth—
An evident civilian, with one boot
Half off, in flight, face white, lungs short of breath.
Out of a barn another soldier comes,
Gun at the ready, finding at his feet
One more old yokel, gone half mad with fear,
Tripped in his path, wild legs up in the air.

Roofs smashed, smoke rising, distant glow of fire,
A woman's thighs splayed open after rape
And lying there still: charred flecks caught in the air,
And caught for ever by a man from Antwerp
Whose style was 'crudely narrative', though 'robust',
According to this scholar, who never knew
What Pieter Snayers saw in 1632.

AT JAMESTOWN

By Greyhound south from Washington's white domes,
Passing low factories and supermarkets,
Along a road where no one ever walks
But touched only by hot and whining rubber,
I reach the first frail enclave of these states.

Jamestown. Its relics dredged from swamp and fever,
It lacks even the substances of ruins
But must be dug for in its lost encampment,
Each scrap and shred and sherd disjected tokens
Of failure never staunched, of pointless landfall.

Imperial peninsula! Beyond
The crammed museum the rich landscape swarms
With cemeteries of cars, the stench of waste
Fanned upward from Virginia's garbage cans,
The sewage of a whole half continent.

Magnolia comes to blossom as the cameras
Snap at these smaller, rarer sediments.
Down the brown estuary fresh water flows,
And far behind it all the prodigal
And violent issue briefly fathered here.

WORM WITHIN

A SOUVENIR from Sicily on the shelf:
A wooden doll carved out of some dark wood,
And crudely carved, for tourists. There it stood
Among the other stuff. Until one night,
Quietly reading to myself, I heard
It speak, or creak—a thin, persistent scratch,
Like the first scrape of a reluctant match,
Or unarticulated word
That made me look for it within myself

As if I talked to myself. But there it was,
Scratching and ticking, an erratic clock
Without a face, something as lifeless as rock
Until its own announcement that it shared
Our life with us. A woodworm, deep inside,
Drilled with its soft mouth through the pitch-stained wood
And like the owl presaging death of good,
Its beak closing as the dynasty died,
It held fear in those infinitesimal jaws.

So—to be practical—we must choose two ways:
Either to have some expert treat the thing
(Trivial, absurd, embarrassing)
Or throw it out, before the infection eats
The doors and floors away: this Trojan horse
In miniature could bring the whole house down,
I think to myself wildly, or a whole town . . .
Why do we do nothing, then, but let its course
Run, ticking, ticking, through our nights and days?

THE BONFIRE

DAY by day, day after day, we fed it
With straw, mown grass, shavings, shaken weeds,
The huge flat leaves of umbrella plants, old spoil
Left by the builders, combustible; yet it
Coughed fitfully at the touch of a match,
Flared briefly, spat flame through a few dry seeds
Like a chain of fireworks, then slumped back to the soil
Smouldering and smoky, leaving us to watch

Only a heavy grey mantle without fire.
This glum construction seemed choked at heart,
The coils of newspaper burrowed into its hulk
Led our small flames into the middle of nowhere,
Never touching its centre, sodden with rot.
Ritual petrol sprinklings wouldn't make it start
But swerved and vanished over its squat brown bulk,
Still heavily sullen, grimly determined not

To do away with itself. A whiff of smoke
Hung over it as over a volcano.
Until one night, late, when we heard outside
A crackling roar, and saw the far field look
Like a Gehenna claiming its due dead.
The beacon beckoned, fierily aglow
With days of waiting, hiding deep inside
Its bided time, ravenous to be fed.

AT THE WINDOW

GREEN bulwark of the chestnut heaves in air
Towards this window, cleaves and tosses spray
From leaf to leaf, its branched and clustered prow
Heavy under the clouds' insistent flow.
Its toppling weight flings higher than the house,
Falling and rising massively to where
A jet goes blundering, roaring on its way
Across a sky obscured with thickened boughs.

Rooted and restless, watching behind glass
Such fierce contenders harmlessly perform
Their rapt compulsions, now I turn away
And face books, papers, furniture, my day
Belittled by the sight, as if my own
Making was measured thus and could not pass
Tests so devised, or cast in such a form.
Each branch is shaken, every leaf is blown.

And so I look again, and find it now
As still and two-dimensional as some
Backcloth from *Hagoromo*, a green tree
In front of which masked men and spirits see
The pattern of their future, unperturbed
And not to be evaded. On one bough
A thrush has settled. Its clear measures come
Across clear lengths of distance, undisturbed.

And they will fall—bird, chestnut, house and all—
As surely as the rain, more quietly
Than the plane's swelling and withdrawing scream,
And gradually, like falling in a dream
Through boughs and clouds that scatter as we float
Downwards on air that holds us as we fall
Towards a landing place we never see,
Bare, treeless, soundless, cloudlessly remote.

CIRCUS

AFTER a wait of about half an hour
The four-piece band (three men in tinsel suits
And a fourth in creased blue serge who pours with sweat)
Strikes up and bashes out some frisky notes
Like automatons. We perch high in the air
On planks, and sniff the dusty animal smell,
And hear the roar
Of lions somewhere outside the tent. Susceptible,
Our two-year-old daughter twirls like a marionette.

Tumblers and clowns and jugglers, women with thighs
Like elephants in tights, a saxophonist
Who plays the thing while standing on his head
In a hat on a table: that such worlds exist
Is new to half this lot, whose shrill applause
Brings on more clowns, more jugglers, who perform
More briskly as the roars
Mount to a brawl of snarls. Thickly the warm
Odours of expectation rise and spread.

A gang of cosmopolitan sinisters
Rig up a wire cage on the trodden sand
A few yards from our faces. Trumpets screech.
Then down a flimsy tunnel comes the sound
Of petulant grunts, the final harbingers
Before at last the six thin mummers slink
Minus their roars
Into the cage. With stale and feline stink
They meekly wait. Their master tortures each.

Smack goes the whip, in goes the little goad:
Up on their stools and boxes sit the six,
Like clowns whose whole art is their awkwardness.
For fifteen minutes they display their tricks,

But by that time the day has been betrayed,
The longed-for unimaginable gone.
Outside, nothing is said
Except by Alice, ecstatically alone,
Who twirls and dances in her happiness.

ENTRY

Died, 1778: *Moses Ozier, son of a woman out of her mind, born in the ozier ground belonging to Mr. Craft.*

CHRISTENED with scripture, eponymously labelled,
You lie so small and shrunken in the verger's tall
Archaic writing. Born in the low water meadows
Down the end of lawns where you would be unlikely to walk
Supposing you'd ever got that far in life, no Pharaoh's daughter
Plucked you out of the bulrushes, for this was Yorkshire
And prophets had stopped being born. Your lunatic mother
Knelt in the rushes and squirmed in her brute pain,
Delivering you up to a damp punishing world
Where the ducks were better off, and the oziers wetly rustled
Sogged down in the marshland owned by Mr. Craft.

It's sense to suppose you lasted a few days
And were buried, gratis, in an unmarked hole at the edge
Of the churchyard, the verger being scrupulous
And not wanting your skinny christened bundle of bones
To lie in unhallowed ground.

                           Poor tiny Moses,
Your white face is a blank, anonymous
Like other people's babies. Almost two hundred years
Since you briefly lay by the cold and placid river,
And nothing but nineteen words as memorial.

I hear you cry in the night at the garden's dark edge.

THE FORESTERS ARMS

No trees in sight except thin spindly things
Giving no shelter to animal or bird,
Not worth the pruning, valueless as fuel,
Bearing no fruit or timber: concrete acreage
Stretches about, grey packaging of soil.
On the hill-gradient no sound is heard
But lorries changing gear; no beat of wings
Of hawk or owl above this global village.
A tanker pumps in someone's Special Ale.

Scragged earth, starved grass, coke litter under rain,
Low sheds and railway sidings—factories
That ease my life with things I do not need
Dictate such stuff. And in among it all,
Its sign new-painted, chrome replacing wood,
At odds with every neighbouring thing it sees,
The Foresters Arms marks out its old domain,
Deaf to the echo of a horn's long call
And sounds of men with axes felling trees.

AT DUNKESWELL ABBEY

BELOW the ford, the stream in flood
Rises and laps the leaf-choked wood
And fallen branches trap thick mud.
Pebbles are swept like slingstones down
Runnels and channels sliced through stone
And in the hollows sink and drown.

On either side broad ramparts hold
The water back from copse and field,
Where a dry earthbank seems to fold
Protectively a hollow space
Of pasture edged with stunted trees
In its inert and curved embrace.

Six hundred years ago, great pike
Grown old in this man-fashioned lake
Swam through its lily clusters like
Dream-presences below the mind.
Dark waters stirred where now I stand
Hearing the distant stream unwind.

The stillness here was made to last.
Whatever shapes survive exist
In some faint diagram of the past,
A sketch-map tentative as those
Robbed walls whose simulacrum lies
In patches summer droughts expose.

One wall still overtops the trees
Beyond the ford, but bramble grows
Round rotten stone. What energies
Persist are harnessed to the stream,
Violent in flood, not curbed or tame,
And hurtling without plan or aim.

REFORMATION

The hazed meadows of England grow over chancels
Where cattle hooves kick up heraldic tiles
And molehills heap their spoils above slumped walls.
The cruck-beamed roofs of refectories nestle under
Sheds and barns, hay piled high where
Augustine and Aquinas chapter by chapter
Were read in these now lapsed pastoral acres.

Small streams wash the smashed crockery of Cistercians.
Stone-plaited carvings are wedged in gable ends
Of farmhouses, springs irrigate robbed chapels
Where all is marsh, reeds meshed among cracked altars.
A buzzard shrieks *yaa-i* in a tall tree,
Plainchant echoing along the valleys.
High hedges stand above spoiled finials.

And Sunday mornings see small meeting houses,
Reformed parishes and tabernacles,
Bethesdas and the whole wide countryside,
All split seven ways in sect and congregation,
Assembling to praise God from whom all blessings
Flow through his derelict priories, abbeys, cells
The afternoon sun will show, faint shadows among fields.

SEA

THIS sea has been going a long time,
Sluicing out gullies, chafing rocks,
Grinding boulders to pebbles, and scouring pebbles
Till the hard white veins stand out.

                                        It lifts its wet tons
Heavily from the low fathoms, it makes nonsense
Of timbers and lobster-pots, it polishes bottles
To frivolous bits of glitter, goes eating on
Through cliffs and headlands, thudding its steady fist
Into igneous layers gone cold after eruptions,
And the litter of low coasts is like confetti to it.

Tides don't tame it, the moon knows that,
Pulling and pushing with a slow, drugged rhythm:
They can't stop those pools and pockets swarming with its fry
When the great thing itself is almost out of sight
Flicking and flickering on the horizon—
It's coming back, it's gathering its windy breath
To stride back up its beaches, to knock again
Heavily hammering at its lost sea-bed
Now calling itself America or Europe,
Names to be carried awhile, till they tumble back
Into the boiling mess that started it all,
Hot seas without vessels, coasts, rocks, fish,
Unmapped, ungovernable, without tidy names.

SEA ANEMONE

Purple guzzler, stomach with fingers,
Or weed-green flaunter of delicate feathers,
You suck like studs to your beached rocks
Glued and tacky to the touch.
Then, underwater, flare tumescent and draw in
The frail shrimps, nervous skeletons, to your gut—
A blunt tube, ravenous.

There is nothing, surely, to be learned from you,
Low feeder, except to know
That eating is all we share, and that the sea
Is happier for you than it is for us:
And it did not need the sea-anemone
To tell us that.

GREEN ISLAND

A SQUAT hummock of sand,
Grass-fringed, pebble-surrounded,
Lifts above tides to be
At lowest ebb of water
A castle for children,
A nook for lovers.

Acres of sand, of seaweed
With slick rubber pods,
Sprawl far out from shore.
Easy to reach the island,
A low trampled place,
Humbled by people.

But the tide moves in,
The bathers dress, the lovers
Walk back hand in hand
To *Mon Plaisir*, the children
Run shouting over pebbles.
The island empties, and fills

In its gullies, its sand courses,
With harsh water, bitter salt,
The weeds lifting the swirl
To the last effort of grass
Topping the trodden mound,
Marking the land's end,
The sea's chosen landmark.

THE COLLECTOR

He must add one more, just one
More pebble to the spread store
Laid out on the shore:
The pink, the green, the black,
The curiously veined, the one
With its graffiti. They lack
The missing one, the inevitable one more.

So he must search another hour
To find it, while on the way
Another dozen must prolong his stay.
Somewhere the ideal shape and shade
Eludes his grasp, escapes his power,
And as his earlier garnerings dry and fade
He adds their mute excuses to delay

The moment when he will
Acknowledge that one more must be
The end of it. The sea
Will not, today, give him that one
He seeks for to perfect the pile.
The hoard bleaches dully in the sun.
He leaves it, pockets empty, hands free.

ELSEWHERE

ELSEWHERE, the autumn wood fills with red leaves
Silently. Worm-casts spill across meadows.
Grass withers. The sun moves west, assigning cold.

Elsewhere, a magpie clacks into the trees.
A kestrel treads on air. The path is thick
With turfed-out snail-shells, and against a gate

A squirrel hangs as hostage. Elsewhere, too,
Smoke drifts across valleys, blossoms above towns
Invested by artillery. Along highways

Drivers hurry to suburbs where lawns lie
Heavy under rain, unmown. Elsewhere children
Are rawly born. And the moon inclines its light

On domes, torn posters, curfew guards. Elsewhere,
You sit on a bed while across the corridor
A scream spirals and jerks, again, again,

Then spins down fast and settles into sobs.

And no elsewhere is here, within your head
Where nothing else is born, or grows, or dies.
Nothing is like this, where the world turns in

And shapes its own alarms, noises, signs,
Its small aggressions and its longer wars,
Its withering, its death. Outside, begins

Whatever shape I choose to give it all
(Clouds ribbed with light, signals I recognize)
But you sit silent, narrowly, in a world

So light I feel it brush my cheek, and fall.

DEAD METAPHORS

A CHILD refusing to be born, carried so long
It smothers the heart, dying as the mother dies.
A scar speaking in cold weather of the flesh it was.
A purlieu of levelled bricks where a house once stood.
A hand reaching out in the dark and closing on nothing.
A stain washed faint, neither wine nor blood.

And it is not a child, because we never met,
Nor is it a scar, because no wound was there,
Nor is it waste ground, because in the empty air
No house was ever built, and our hands were closed like fists
Keeping what we had, and whatever we spilt
Gathers like dry stuff a vague girl dusts.

SWITZERLAND

In a valley in Switzerland a brass band marches.
The dapper chalets twinkle in the sun
Among the meadows and the well-drilled larches
And watercourses where streams briskly run.

Bravely the little drums pretend their thunder
To far-off crags whose melting snow brings down
A rattle of small pebbles buried under
Drifts deeper than the church spire in the town.

The soldier-citizens of the canton practise
Before an audience of sheep and cows.
As for the real thing, the simple fact is
Each keeps a well-oiled rifle in his house.

Duchies and principalities have fathered
These drums and cornets under angrier skies,
Bucolic bellicosities which gathered
The Ruritanian airs of paradise

Into a clockwork joke envious Europe
Could laugh at, play in, patronize, ignore,
As, poised between the saddle and the stirrup,
The Switzer was acknowledged as a bore.

The peaceable kingdom rests on marks and dollars
Beside the lake at Zurich, lined with banks,
Far from the towns draped with insurgent colours
Whose dawn breaks with the grinding tread of tanks.

The Alpine avalanche holds back this summer
Its fragile tons, and watches from the height
The nimble piper and the strutting drummer
Putting the valley's herbivores to flight.

SPRING

HEAVY the obdurate fell weight of snow,
Heavy the season's burden as the year
Accumulates thick ice no sun can thaw,
Raising its long black granite frontier.
But wanly, slowly, piecemeal down below
Something has found the winter's hidden flaw.

Under a lip of snow a tongue of water
Licks at crushed twigs, spun pebbles, shifting mud,
And in the ooze a beaked blue-headed flower
Thrusts up into the loosening spring: a flood
Of blossom hangs above the glacier
And breaks in showers across the still dark wood.

NOW

So many of them, and so many still to come:
They crowd the pavements, pour from the discreet chimneys
Of crematoria, advance with arms linked
Down avenues, protesting or celebrating,
Are spaded under sand and rock and clay,
And still come young and bloodily among us.
It will go on, nothing can stop it happening.

Given that first great sunburst, and the mindless time
Moving towards cell and union, coelocanth and midge,
What could prevent sparse tribes of hominids
Drifting like winged seeds over the land-masses
And ending up here, on the second floor
Of a house facing south, one Sunday in October,
Caught in the middle years and counting syllables?

NOTE ON THE BLUE NOTEBOOK

In the blue notebook, some pages are detached:
15 to 42. On either side
The cancelled versions run muddily across
Broad foolscap sheets, struck through and scribbled over.
But at the spine two furred tufts mark the loss
Of something which the poet wished to hide,
Or so we judge. The right-hand page shows scratched
Impressions, some scored deep: *betrayed, guilt, lover.*

Nothing at front or back gives up a clue
Of what the abandoned poems were about,
Except the ambiguous words uninked though etched.
Up to 14, his monologue on hope:
From 43, some fragments, unattached.
Biographers have hedged all round with doubt,
Critics have called this false, the other true,
Orthographers have used a microscope.

On grey steel shelves, in dustless libraries,
The bound books neatly stand. In fireproof stacks
Notebooks and worksheets rank in numbered files.
The bibliography is well in hand,
The variorum measures out his styles.
Yet by some thirty pages the world lacks
His central, perhaps crucial, testimonies:
Deliberate, bitter; or ravished and unplanned.

GENERATION GAP

OUTSIDE, on the dark campus lawns,
An apoplectic howling goes
On and on, while inside dons
Sit glumly listening to the news
In nordic-brutalist maisonettes.

Outside, the grammar-school head boy
Now on a trip to God-knows-where
Shrieks for ten demons to destroy
The demons tearing his fuzzed hair.
The nuclear family goes to bed.

And quiet at last, as midnight comes,
The lowland mists creep through the grass
Towards the functional dark rooms
And leave a cloud upon the glass
That lasts till daylight, and beyond.

INSCRIPTIONS

KNICKERS Fisher has been at work again,
Using a compass point on the closet door,
But he's a miniaturist whose main concern
Is altogether different from the team
Exhibiting on the wall by the railway line:
SMASH THE STATE stands six feet high or more
In strong black paint where the track crosses the stream—
Opposites in the field of graphic design.

And in the middle scale are the stone slabs
Pecked out by masons dead these hundred years,
Gravestones along the passage to the town:
They make their claims too, with a different voice,
But still in hope and expectation. They
Exhort and yearn and stiffly mask the fears
Of men with large obsessions and small choice,
Burdened with flesh and law till judgement day.

A HAIKU YEARBOOK

Snow in January
Looking for ledges
To hide in unmelted.

February evening:
A cold puddle of petrol
Makes its own rainbow.

Wind in March:
No leaves left
For its stiff summons.

April sunlight:
Even the livid bricks
Muted a little.

Wasp in May
Storing his venom
For a long summer.

Morning in June:
On the sea's horizon
A white island, alone.

July evening:
Sour reek of beer
Warm by the river.

August morning:
A squirrel leaps and
Only one branch moves.

September chestnuts:
Falling too early,
Split white before birth.

44

October garden:
At the top of the tree
A thrush stabs an apple.

November morning:
A whiff of cordite
Caught in the leaf mould.

Sun in December:
In his box of straw
The tortoise wakes.

THE LIFE AND DEATH OF THE
PINE PROCESSIONARY

THIS is a garden for the cultivation of death.
Here under glass the leaves and pine-branches have only one
    purpose:
to harbour sickness, to carry disease, to destroy—
and *I* have been marked down.
The name they give me is the Pine Processionary, and I am
    legion.

In the pine forests of Provence I live in my thick and tangled
    colonies
for a little while longer.

In Spring, my colonies wake one day
to discover a place where I must change in some way.
What I am looking for
is powdery soil or sand, granules in the sun,
where I must bury myself. In procession
I spin a silken thread, each to each,
to mark a clear path for my slow progress,
my metamorphosis.

But some must fall by the way, for we have enemies:
the hot acids of the ant, sharper than his sharp beak,
spill into me and madden me. From my clefts and segments
I volley out my lances, my brittle hairs,
in a fine poisonous dust. Some must fall, ants and caterpillars.
My tough survivors start out again, and then
huddle together, ready for another kind of burial.

Each weaves his shroud, shutting out the light,
mimicking death, a phoenix bedded down
in sand and silk, not fire.

I am beginning to be born again,
my head a steel-hard drill, tunnelling upwards,

scattering sand-grains and pebbles, flailing the earth aside,
ponderous, blind, earthbound,
a brown lump of damp tissue,
heaving myself over the punishing earth.

But the air is my nurse, and the sun. They draw
my wings into life, I stretch, I rise up, I move
tentative, painful, suddenly aware
of constriction moving away, of a new power
which is not wholly mine, my whole purpose in life
to propagate
and, that done, to die again:

the brief clumsy act, and then our separate deaths—
the male, shaken and feeble, utterly spent;
the female, a little while longer to lay her eggs,
then also twitching, dying.

Even those eggs, packed tight among the pine needles,
are vulnerable. The cricket is hungry for them.

Gulped in succulent mandibles,
the prodigal waste of life is measured out.

But enough survive. After a month, those of us left
hatch out into a world of air and food.

Spin and pirouette,
peer and bob and nod and toddle,
walk the silk tightrope of the silk thread,
dance, for a while, dance.

After the fiery ant and the predatory cricket,
the obscene lunging fly, choked and brimming
with a sluiceful of white eggs, choosing our youngest
as compost for her own young, who will feed
through the tunnels of our bodies, leaving some
mere husks, the dead receptacles of the living,
hosts for parasites.

But again, my will is to survive:
enough of us to spin our white cities
safe against all enemies we know,
or have known until now.

These are our forests, empires of sustenance,
ripe for our feasting, the delicate shoots of pine
laid out in liberal acres, a whole emporium
ripe for our gluttony.

The sweetness of this food, soft and hard!
Eat, eat,
till our cities bulge with our full bodies,
the trees where we munch great banquets of the night,
a steady roar of appetite, of greed.

At dawn, bloated, we lace and loop ourselves
back to our cities, finding our gorged way
with threads spun in the evening in the trees.

And when the Spring returns
the other trees, the trees we do not know,
put on their buds and leaves and live again.
But the pines have been consumed, are in our bellies.

Now, after the ravages of the ant,
the cricket and the fly
time for a new and deadlier enemy: man.
Man, to protect his forests, builds a forest
under roofs, under glass, among white and sterile things
that never knew life at all:
an abattoir for insects.

My diseased body, its guts swollen with the one
virus wholly my own:
the long incision lays it bare, to let leak out
my innermost enemy, a milky stuff
crammed with my own death, to be multiplied,
a virus . . .

                    a virus isolated, magnified,
a many-sided weapon, sharp-edged, focused
on my annihilation,
to be crushed into liquid, agitated, then
rendered to fragments, fed to me at last—
so that I eat my death and breed it too.

Five weeks, and the virus has destroyed all those
fed from the poisoned twigs, and yet no other creature
will die because of this. Mild to all other creatures,
to us it spells out death.

So from the slopes of Mont Ventoux, the slopes
which our great cities colonized and scoured,
men gather a miniature forest of death, and feed
half a million of us, the healthy ones—
picked for our health, but picked to kill the rest.

Each nest we build, each colony, shuts in
two hundred caterpillars, all condemned.

Where once we danced, we hang—a parody
of all our dancing youthful ancestors.
The dead are counted,
a monotonous declension, a catalogue of deaths.

From flesh to liquid to dust, a lethal powder mixed
to put an end to all of us: a mere
forty tons, they say, to exterminate
the greedy armies, the eaters of the pines.

Over the hills,
over the pine forests, the great bird flies
over and over, poisoning us alone.

The epidemic spreads, the corpses hang
dustily in the trees, to be swept away
by the Spring winds, turned to dust, made dust
by dust from our own bodies.

49

Over the hills,
over the pine forests, the great bird flies
over and over, poisoning us alone
as the dust swirls and falls in its long, deliberate skeins.

The procession halts. The processionary dies.
The hills remain, and the forests, and the men.

POINTS

This is the arrow which I, a warrior, shot,
Lifting up the bow-end:
Let it remind those who find it
To talk of me for ever.

KASA KANAMURA (fl. A.D. 715–33)

I

AT the Yoshino Palace, in the fifth month,
Kasa Kanamura, laureate of Nara,
Anthology compiler, brocaded and pale,
Lifted the supple bow, drew breath,
Drew back the bowstring with the bamboo arrow
And smoothly let flow forth the tip of bright metal.

It lay where it fell, away from the target,
And lay as he left it.
                    He, struck (like no target)
With the thought of it lying
Where it had fallen
To stay there . . . And so
'I, a warrior' flowed smooth from his brush
On the scroll before him, as he fingered the syllables
And spoke without breath
And walked to his grave,
Who had seen the quick torrents
Shouldering the mountains
And the tumbling cascades
Race by the pala e
(Stout-timbered, stone-walled) and
'In dread of their majesty'
Had sunk in his mind
To the rock-bed below,
And had stood, his mind floating
Like Mitsune after him . . .
Arrow, bright arrow
Fallen, there.

II

Fluted like this one, no longer than the first joint
Of my little finger, the bright bronze burnished
Under the weathers of twelve hundred years:
And not among grave goods, with cuirass and bracelet
Or gilded helmet or suppliant vessels,
But lodged in the thick grass of a humid summer
To lie under plaited leaves, under welts of mud,
Pressed down, trodden under, lost where it landed
In a curve out of air from bow, gut, pressure
Of fingers against arc of muscle, of air . . .

III

Today is the anniversary
Of Gamae, Nasamonian, one who ate locusts
And slept in the tombs of his ancestors
So as to dream prophecies:
Today such a man died
Somewhere in the desert north of the Psylli
Who were buried as they marched
To vanquish the South Wind.

And today, too, the anniversary
Of Arx, miner of obsidian,
Who lugged the black nuggets from a cliff on Lipari
To be fashioned by other men: and of Oyu,
Carver of bone amulets in Hokkaido:
Of Tacan, acolyte, of Chichen Itza—all
Inventions, you take it rightly, type-names of the nameless
Whose artefacts are numbered, labelled, filed
In corridors, in dustless libraries,
Mapped by distribution, plotted by computer,
Under whose alluvial tonnage the nostrils drew in air
And suffocated at the mortal touch.

Humbled among trophies, mementoes not only of death.

IV

At Karnak the lintels
At Thebes the pediments
At Antioch the walls
At Nineveh the pavements
At Konarak the platforms
At Sidon the bollards
At Troy the columns
At Angkor the terraces . . .
Yoshino fallen, the thousand ages
Drawn to the point of the tip of an arrow.

V

And at Augila the dates
The salt hills gushing water
And the crying of women
And Ghirza buried:
Acreage of stones
Above wells of water
And a flake of volcano
Flashing black fire,
Worked with the thumb
Shaped into sharpness
The tooth of the serpent
Hardened to stone
The flail of the scorpion
Petrified, polished

The armature perished
The poison crushed
To crystals of dust.

VI

In the palm of my left hand
Among the unread lines
The arrowhead lies cupped:
Its point, still sharp, defines

Its purpose, its abrupt
Quiddity. To end
Function is not to kill,
Nor lack of it to die.
The thousand ages cram
Survival's narrow way
With fragments. What I am
Emerges from the rubble.

VII

A topography of debris—clay, stone, bronze—
Dry hills of Mamelukes, Ghadames slagheaps,
The tells of Troy, the tip of Aberfan,
The mounds and spills at boundaries, beyond limits,
Smoking like Golgotha
                        as the ash descends
Sealing the thrown waste, the scoured junk,
Burying the scourings, embalming the long lost.
                            No sudden blast of cobalt
In the revelations of August, the fleshprint
                            shadowed on stone
As ghost presence, instant eidolon, but
A longer dying, a protracted chapter
Of accidents and discarded product:
The slaughter of utensils, the annihilation of weapons,
Carcases of tools, scattering of stones,
Lifted into the air by the grovelling shovel, and held
Here in the obsolete point that missed the target to
'Remind those who find it
                        to talk of me forever.'

VIII

And so it does,
Though not as you meant it,
Not knowing beyond Nara
The islands and mountains
Or seeing forever

Stretch to this point. Yet
Your poem contains
Its own assurance,
A blind inheritance
We share, in going on
Because we must,
Surviving destruction,
Valuing the dust.